Date: 02/13/12

J BIO MAUER
Zuehlke, Jeffrey,
Joe Mauer /

Joe Mauer

By Jeffrey Zuehlke

AMAZING ATHLETES

Lerner Publications Company • Minneapolis

For Graham, Saint Paul kid; and for Jon Fishman, the greatest left-handed-hitting editor ever

Lerner Publications Company
A division of Lerner Publishing Group, Inc.
241 First Avenue North
Minneapolis, MN 55401 U.S.A.

Website address: www.lernerbooks.com

Library of Congress Cataloging-in-Publication Data

Zuehlke, Jeffrey, 1968–
    Joe Mauer / by Jeffrey Zuehlke.
        p.   cm. — (Amazing athletes)
    Includes bibliographical references and index.
    ISBN 978-0-8225-8835-1 (lib. bdg : alk. paper)
    1. Mauer, Joseph Patrick, 1983—Juvenile literature. 2. Baseball players—United States—Biography—Juvenile literature. 3. Minnesota Twins (Baseball team)—Biography—Juvenile literature. I. Title.
GV865.M376Z84 2008
796.357092—dc22 [B]   2007030119

Manufactured in the United States of America
1 2 3 4 5 6 – DP – 13 12 11 10 09 08

TABLE OF CONTENTS

Joe Mauer gets a hit in the fourth inning of the last game of the 2006 season.

MAKING HISTORY

Joe Mauer was nervous. The Minnesota Twins **catcher** had a chance to make baseball history. He was trying to do something no **American League (AL)** catcher had done before. Could he pull it off?

Joe and the Twins were playing their last game of the 2006 **Major League Baseball (MLB) regular season**. Joe was in the hunt for the AL **batting title**. This award goes to the player with the league's best **batting average**. No catcher had ever won the AL title before.

Joe started the game with a .346 average. But New York Yankees shortstop Derek Jeter was close behind at .344. Joe needed to get a few hits to make sure he won the title.

Jeter and the Yankees were playing in Toronto against the Blue Jays. Joe was playing in the Metrodome in Minneapolis, Minnesota. He had about 45,000 Twins fans cheering him on.

In Toronto, Jeter got a hit in his first **at-bat**. This meant that both Joe and Jeter had .346 averages. The pressure was on the Twins catcher.

Derek Jeter gets a hit against the Blue Jays in one of the last games of the season.

Joe kisses his bat before heading to the plate.

Joe struck out in his first at-bat. He *really* needed to get some hits. Joe's second at-bat came in the fourth inning. The crowd roared as he smacked a base hit to left field.

Joe had a chance to hit again in the fifth inning. He smacked a single to left field! This raised Joe's average to .348. Joe's last at-bat came in the seventh. He failed to get a hit. He finished the season with a .347 average.

Joe is the only AL catcher to win the batting title. But two National League (NL) catchers have done it. The last NL catcher to win the title was Ernie Lombardi of the Boston Braves. Lombardi won it way back in 1942.

But Jeter also failed to get another hit in his game. Jeter finished with a .343 average. Joe had won the batting title! The Twins and their fans celebrated.

Joe is usually cool and calm. He doesn't get too excited about things. But this day was different.

"I've never been that nervous in my life," Joe said after the game, smiling ear to ear. "I'm feeling pretty good right now."

Saint Paul is the capital of Minnesota. It is across the Mississippi River from Minneapolis, the home of the Twins.

NOT YOUR AVERAGE JOE

Joseph Patrick Mauer was born on April 19, 1983, in Saint Paul, Minnesota. He was born into a family of talented athletes. His father, uncles, and older brothers were all good at sports.

From an early age, Joe loved baseball. "I guess as soon as I picked up a bat [at the age of two], I didn't let go," says Joe. Even as a small kid, he showed talent. In fact, he was kicked off of his local T-ball team because he was too good. "They wanted me out of the league because I hit the ball too hard," says Joe.

Joe grew up in Saint Paul. Like many Minnesota kids, he was a big fan of the Twins. Twins legend Kirby Puckett was his favorite player. Joe dreamed of playing for his hometown team.

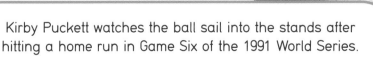

Kirby Puckett watches the ball sail into the stands after hitting a home run in Game Six of the 1991 World Series.

As a kid, Joe spent much of his free time playing sports. He was good at football and basketball. But baseball was his favorite sport. He and his older brothers played stickball on the street in front of their house. "We'd get out there with a broom handle and tennis ball and play," says Joe.

The hitting tool that Joe's dad made was so successful that the Mauers decided to sell it to the public. The Mauer Quick Swing is one of the most popular hitting tools on the market.

Joe's dad invented a special tool to help his boys practice their hitting. It was a V-shaped pipe on a stand. The batter dropped a ball into one end of the pipe. The ball rolled out the other end. The batter swung at the ball as it came out. The boys used it to practice for hours and hours.

Joe's dad, Jake Mauer II *(right)*, stands with his father, Jake Mauer I. Joe's dad spent many years coaching his sons' teams.

The tool helped Joe perfect his swing. "He'd bring it into the gym three or four times a week," said one of his baseball coaches. "And the other kids couldn't come close using baseballs and bats. Meanwhile, Joe was hitting golf balls with a piece of pipe."

Joe keeps his eye on the ball as he bats for his high school team, the Cretin-Derham Hall Raiders.

THREE-SPORT STAR

By the time he reached high school, everyone could see that Joe had special talent. It looked as if he had a future as a pro athlete. But Joe was a star in football, basketball, and baseball. Which sport would he choose?

By his **sophomore** year, he was getting a lot of attention from pro baseball teams. "We had been tracking him since he was about fifteen," said then Twins general manager Terry Ryan. "Left-handed hitting catchers are tough to come [by]. And there's no question that Joe was talented."

Joe went to the same high school as MLB Hall of Fame player Paul Molitor.

Meanwhile, Joe was the best player on his basketball team too. For his **junior** and **senior** seasons, he was named All-State in basketball. But he was an even better football player. As the star **quarterback**, Joe led his Cretin-Derham Hall Raiders team to two state championship games. The Raiders won the title in Joe's junior season in 1999.

The team lost the title game in 2000. But Joe still had a spectacular season. He threw for more than 3,000 yards. He also threw 41 touchdown passes. Joe even set a state record with seven touchdown passes in one game.

Joe ended his high school football career as the top player in the country. He was named the 2000 High School Football Player of the Year. Joe was even named as a star of the future in *Sports Illustrated* magazine.

Joe gets ready to make a throw as quarterback for his high school team.

All the top colleges wanted him to play quarterback for them. He got calls from the University of Miami, the University of Michigan, and other schools.

Joe wasn't sure what he wanted to do. He still had a season of high school baseball to play. But if he wanted to play college football, he had to make a decision. Joe signed a letter to play for the Florida State Seminoles. But he could change his mind later.

Joe's last high school baseball season was just as good as his football season. **Scouts** from pro

Joe struck out only once in his entire high school baseball career. "It was junior year, and it was in the state tournament. I came back to the bench and everybody thought something was wrong with me."

Joe played catcher on his high school baseball team.

baseball teams watched all of his games. "I just remember coming out of the locker room and you'd see all these scouts over there," said Joe. "Every team represented, almost every day."

At the end of the season, he was named the top high school baseball player in the country. No athlete had ever been named the best baseball and football player before.

So what would Joe do? Would he play football or baseball? He wasn't totally sure.

Joe puts on a Twins jersey after being picked first in the Major League Baseball draft on June 5, 2001.

WHERE WILL JOE GO?

Meanwhile, the Major League Baseball **draft** was coming up in June 2001. All the teams would be selecting players.

Deep down, Joe wanted to play baseball. He decided that if a team made him a top pick, he would play baseball. To make things more exciting, the Minnesota Twins had the first pick in the draft that year.

When draft day came, the Twins took Joe with the first pick. "It was just an unbelievable feeling," he said.

"Everything worked out perfectly," said Joe's older brother Bill. "Joe wanted to be a Twin. He didn't want to go anywhere else. The Twins are his team."

Like most players, Joe started his pro career in the **minor leagues**. His first team was the Elizabethton Twins of the Appalachian League. He moved to Tennessee, far away from home. Luckily, he already knew one of his teammates. The Twins had drafted his brother Jake that same summer. Both played for Elizabethton in 2001.

Joe's first season was amazing. His batting average was an incredible .400! He was named the league's top **prospect**.

By his third year as a pro, Joe was ready for the big leagues. He began the 2004 season as the Twins' starting catcher. He was just 21 years old.

Joe's fans hold up a banner for his major-league debut on April 5, 2004.

Joe got a hit on the first day. He looked set to have a good season, but he hurt his knee two days later. The knee took a long time to heal. Joe ended up playing in just 35 games.

He came into 2005 healthy and ready to play. He had a strong season. Joe played in 131 games. He finished with a team-best .294 batting average and 26 **doubles**.

By this time, Joe was already one of the Twins' most popular players. Fans loved his great hitting and his humble attitude. "He's just a good baseball player," says his manager, Ron Gardenhire. "He's . . . a good combination of a person and a player."

After the draft, Joe signed a contract for $5 million. "Everybody was wondering what kind of car I would get. I'm not a flashy guy. I got a Chevy truck."

Joe waits for the ball during a game against the Chicago White Sox.

CATCHING ON

There is a reason why only a few catchers have won batting titles. Catcher is probably the most difficult position in baseball. "[Catching] is tough physically, but also mentally," says Joe.

"Say you play in the outfie[ld]. [Then] you're not in on every pit[ch as] little. With catching, the pl[ay...]

Catchers take a lot of pu[nishment at] the plate. They get hit with [wild] pitches. All the aches and p[ains can] make it tough to hit well.

So why d[o...] "Catche[r...] like [...]

Joe tags out Kansas City Royals player Emil Brown at home plate.

es Joe play such a tough position?
r is a position of responsibility. And I
running the game, helping our pitchers
and helping our team win."

Joe was ready to take it to the next level in 2006. He started out the season strong. He hit .316 in the first month. Then Joe's hitting took off. He batted .386 in May. But he was just getting started.

After a poor start to the season, the Twins came alive in June. First baseman Justin Morneau started smashing home runs. Superstar pitcher Johan Santana was almost unbeatable. And Joe just kept on hitting. He hit an unbelievable .452 average in June.

On June 7, the Twins were 11½ games behind the Detroit Tigers in the AL **Central Division**. But Minnesota went on to win 71 of

Joe hands the ball to pitcher Johan Santana during a game against the Kansas City Royals in 2006.

their next 104 games. They won the AL Central title on the last day of the season!

As the **playoffs** started, many people said the Twins had a good chance of winning the World Series. But it didn't turn out that way. The Twins lost to the Oakland A's in the first round of the playoffs. But it was a great season overall. Morneau won the AL **Most Valuable Player Award** and Santana won the AL **Cy Young Award**.

Even though they lost in the playoffs, the Twins knew they had a special player in Joe Mauer. So before the 2007 season, they signed him to a new contract. The team agreed to pay

Joe gets a hit against the Seattle Mariners during a 2007 game at the Metrodome.

Joe $33 million over the next four seasons!

Joe and his teammates came into 2007 ready for another super season.

Joe says his favorite food is lasagna. *Guitar Hero* is his favorite video game.

"Everything was great last year, but it's a new year and I have to go out there and try to do it again," said Joe. But when the season started, the Twins struggled. Joe had a hard time staying healthy. He missed a lot of games because of injuries. Meanwhile, the Cleveland Indians ran away with the AL Central.

Joe is a big star on his hometown team. But he doesn't let his fame go to his head. He remains humble. And he keeps working hard to get better. "I'm just more low-key, I guess. I would rather be one of those guys that just goes out there and does his job, and that's that."

Selected Career Highlights

2007   Signed a four-year, $33 million contract with the Twins
Hit an inside-the-park home run in a July 21 game
   against the Los Angeles Angels of Anaheim
Finished the season with a batting average of .293

2006   Became the first AL catcher to win the batting title, with a
   .347 average
Helped lead the Twins to their fourth AL Central Division title
   in five years
Named AL Player of the Month for June
Named to first MLB All-Star Game
Hit 13 home runs

2005   Had 144 hits in 131 games for a .294 batting average
Had three 4-hit games
Had a 9-game hitting streak and an 8-game hitting
   streak

2004   Played in his first MLB game
Got his first MLB hit in his first MLB game
Got four hits in a game for the first time, against Kansas City on
   July 7

2003   Played for the Fort Myers Miracle and the New Britain Rock Cats in
   the minor leagues
Finished the season with a .338 batting average—best among all
   minor-league catchers
Named Minor League Player of the Year by *Baseball America*
Named Twins Minor League Player of the Month for July
Ranked best prospect in the Eastern League and Florida State
   League

2002   Played for the Quad City River Bandits in the Midwest League
Selected to the Midwest League All-Star Team

2001   First player taken in the 2001 MLB draft
Hit .400 in first minor-league season for the Elizabethton Twins
Named Twins Minor League Player of the Month for August after
   hitting .411
Rated top prospect in the Appalachian League
Named top catching prospect in baseball by *Baseball America*
   magazine

Glossary

American League (AL): one of MLB's two leagues. The American League has 14 teams, including the Minnesota Twins, New York Yankees, Boston Red Sox, Detroit Tigers, Chicago White Sox, and others.

at-bat: a chance to hit at home plate

batting average: a statistic that judges a player's success at hitting the ball. For example, if a hitter gets 3 hits in 10 at-bats, the batting average would be .300.

batting title: an award that goes to the hitter with the best batting average in the league at the end of the regular season

catcher: a position in baseball. The catcher squats behind the plate and catches pitches. The catcher also helps the pitcher choose which pitches to throw and is responsible for throwing out base runners who are trying to steal bases.

Central Division: one of the three groups that make up the American League. The AL Central is made up of the Chicago White Sox, Cleveland Indians, Detroit Tigers, Kansas City Royals, and Minnesota Twins.

Cy Young Award: an award given out each year to the best pitcher in each of the major leagues

doubles: hits in which the batter is able to reach second base safely

draft: a yearly event in which teams take turns selecting players from a group

junior: a third-year high school or college student

Major League Baseball (MLB): the top group of professional men's baseball teams in North America. MLB is divided into the National League and the American League.

minor leagues: groups of teams in which players improve their skills and prepare to move to the majors

Most Valuable Player Award: an award given out each year to the best player in each of the major leagues

playoffs: a series of games played after the regular season to determine a championship

prospect: a player experts believe will be a good MLB player

quarterback: a position in football whose main job is to lead the offense and throw passes

regular season: the regular schedule for a season. Each MLB team plays 162 regular season games. The top eight teams go to the playoffs.

scouts: people whose job it is to watch players and judge their talent and skills

senior: a fourth-year high school or college student

sophomore: a second-year high school or college student

Further Reading & Websites

Briand, Kevin. *The Baseball Book: A Young Player's Guide to Baseball*. Richmond Hills, ONT: Firefly Books, 2003.

Donovan, Sandy. *Derek Jeter*. Minneapolis: Lerner Publications Company, 2004.

Kelly, James. *Baseball*. New York: DK Publishing, 2005.

Zuehlke, Jeffrey. *Johan Santana*. Minneapolis: Lerner Publications Company, 2007.

Joe Mauer Fan Club
http://www.joemauerfanclub.com
Learn more about Joe and his great career from his fan club site.

Joe Mauer's Baseball Blog
http://www.joemauer.com
Get hitting tips, and see how Joe's season is going from his official website.

Joe Mauer's Quick Swing Batting Aids
http://www.mauersquickswing.com
Learn more about the tool that Joe used to become a great hitter.

Minnesota Twins: The Official Site
http://minnesota.twins.mlb.com
The Minnesota Twins official site has all the latest news about the Twins and Joe Mauer.

Official MLB site
http://www.mlb.com
The official site of Major League Baseball provides up-to-date news and statistics of all 30 major-league teams and every major-league player.

Sports Illustrated for Kids
http://www.sikids.com
The *Sports Illustrated for Kids* website covers all sports, including baseball.

Index

Photo Acknowledgments

The images in this book are used with the permission of: AP Photo/Tom Olmscheid, p. 4; © Anthony J. Causi/Icon SMI, p. 6; © Marlin Levison/ Minneapolis Star Tribune/ZUMA Press, p. 7; © Steven Dahlman/ SuperStock, p. 9; AP Photo/Jim Mone, pp. 10, 18, 20; © Carlos Gonzalez/ Minneapolis Star Tribune/ZUMA Press, p. 12; © Vince Muzik/Icon SMI, pp. 13, 17; © Dawn Villella/St. Paul Pioneer Press, p. 15; © Ron Vesely/MLB Photos via Getty Images, p. 22; AP Photo/Ed Zurga, p. 23; AP Photo/Charlie Riedel, p. 25; © Bryan C. Singer/Icon SMI, p. 26; © Jim McIsaac/Getty Images, p. 28.

Front Cover: © Bruce Kluckhohn